SIBERIAN TIGER

GIANTS AMONG US

Jason Cooper

Rourke Book Co., Inc.
Vero Beach, Florida 32964

Edited by Pamela J.P. Schroeder

NOV 0 3 1998

PHOTO CREDITS
All photos © Lynn M. Stone

Library of Congress Cataloging-in-Publication Data
Cooper, Jason, 1942-
    Siberian tiger / by Jason Cooper.
        p. cm. — (Giants among us)
    Includes index.
    Summary: Describes the physical characteristics, behavior,
and dangers faced by the large, rare cats that live in Siberia
and Manchuria.
    ISBN 1-55916-186-8
    1. Tigers—Juvenile literature. 2. Tigers—Russia—Siberia—
Juvenile literature. [1. Tigers. 2. Endangered species. 3. Rare
animals.] I. Title. II. Series: Cooper, Jason, 1942-
Giants among us.
QL737.C23C675   1997
599.756—dc21   96-52095
                                        CIP
                                        AC

Printed in the USA

TABLE OF CONTENTS

THE SIBERIAN TIGER

The Siberian tiger is an awesome mix of might and beauty. This giant cat is like dynamite in gift wrapping.

Behind the handsome, furry face is a master **predator** (PRED a tor), or hunter. The Siberian tiger is amazingly powerful and quick. It climbs, swims, runs, and leaps with ease.

The Siberian tiger has a predator's keen senses, deadly teeth, and sharp, curved claws. No animal on Earth has better weapons for the hunt.

Siberian tigers have wider muzzles and longer, lighter-colored fur than their tiger cousins.

THE BIGGEST OF BIG CATS

The Siberian tiger is the biggest of big cats. A big male may stand 4 feet (1.2 meters) tall at its shoulders. It can be 13 feet (3.9 m) from its nose to the tip of its tail.

Wild Siberian tigers weigh up to 680 pounds (306 kilograms). Siberian tigers in zoos grow even heavier.

A Siberian tiger can drag its **prey** (PRAY) more than 1/4 mile (.4 kilometers).

The great Siberian, or Amur, tiger is the largest of the world's big cats.

WHERE SIBERIAN TIGERS LIVE

The last few wild Siberian tigers live in southeast Siberia, in Russia, and Manchuria, in China.

The tigers live in rugged country—hills, valleys, and forests. Winters in the tigers' homelands are as mighty as the big cats themselves. Snow lies several feet deep and temperatures drop to -30° Fahrenheit (-35°C).

Siberian tigers overcome winter with long, thick fur and a 2-inch (50-centimeter) layer of fat for warmth.

Siberian tigers live where winter snows are deep and temperatures are bitterly cold.

CUBS, THE BABY TIGERS

A female Siberian tiger usually has a family of two or three cubs. She raises them by herself. They stay with her for two to four years. By watching their mother, the playful cubs, or kittens, learn tiger skills. They learn how and where to find food. They learn how to hide and when to flee.

At birth, a cub weighs no more than 3 pounds (1.4 kg). By age two, the cub may weigh 400 pounds (180 kg)!

Wild Siberian tiger cubs are raised by their mothers in Manchuria and Siberia.

Long, thick fur and a layer of fat keep Siberian tigers toasty warm when snow flies.

For a Siberian tiger, sliding downhill without a sled seems to be great fun.

PREDATOR AND PREY

Siberian tiger cubs are raised to be predators. They live on the prey they kill.

Most of the time, tigers kill large animals, such as wild boar, red deer, sika deer, and bears. Like most cats, Siberian tigers **stalk** (STAWK) prey before attacking it. After making a kill, the tiger may eat 90 pounds (41 kg) before hiding the leftovers for later.

Siberian tigers, like most cats, carefully stalk their prey before attacking it.

SIBERIAN TIGER HABITS

Hunting is hard work. Most attacks fail and the tiger's prey escapes. Sometimes tigers can't find prey. A Siberian tiger may walk 37 miles (60 km) a day to find a meal.

Siberian tigers hunt in daylight and darkness. They use their eyes and ears to find prey.

Adult tigers usually stay away from each other. Each tiger travels in a huge home **territory** (TER rih tor ee). It marks the boundaries with urine and droppings. The marks are "No Trespassing" signs to other tigers.

Siberian tigers looking for prey may travel a long way.

SIBERIAN TIGER COUSINS

The Siberian tiger's closest cousins are the tigers in other, warmer parts of Asia.

Siberian tigers are slightly different. They have longer, lighter-colored fur. They also have wider muzzles and greater size than other tigers.

Bengal tigers of India weigh up to 600 pounds (270 kg). Other tigers, however, are much smaller than the Bengal or Siberian.

Tigers are closely related to lions, leopards, jaguars, and perhaps the snow leopard. Together, these great predators make up the "big cats."

Bengal tigers are smaller and darker than Siberians. Bengals live in warm places so they cool off in rivers and lakes.

PEOPLE AND SIBERIAN TIGERS

Wild tigers throughout Asia are very rare. They are **endangered** (en DANE jerd) animals because they are in danger of **extinction** (ex TINKT shun), disappearing forever.

No one knows how many Siberian tigers live in the wild. The number may be less than 200.

People kill Siberian tigers because they fear them. They also kill them for their fur, bones, and body parts.

In some parts of China, people believe that tiger flesh and bones are powerful medicines.

Yawning, a Siberian tiger at Chicago's Brookfield Zoo shows off its fearsome teeth. More Siberian tigers live in zoos than in the wild.

SAVING SIBERIAN TIGERS

Russia and China don't allow tiger hunting. However, **poachers** (POH churz) still hunt Siberian tigers.

Poachers are criminals who kill animals even though it is against the law. Poachers sell tiger products for a lot of money.

People in North America cannot buy or sell tiger products. In some countries, though, like Taiwan, people openly sell tiger parts in markets.

If poaching is not stopped, the greatest of the big cats will disappear in the wild.

Glossary

endangered (en DANE jerd) — in danger of no longer existing, very rare

extinction (ex TINKT shun) — no longer existing, when a kind of plant or animal disappears forever

poacher (POH chur) — a person who hunts and kills animals that are protected by law

predator (PRED a tor) — an animal that hunts other animals for food

prey (PRAY) — an animal that is hunted by another animal for food

stalk (STAWK) — hunting by moving slowly and quietly toward prey

territory (TER rih tor ee) — the area an animal calls "home" and defends

INDEX